September

Julie Murray

Abdo
MONTHS
Kids

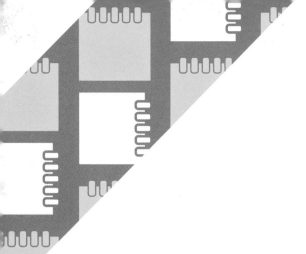

abdopublishing.com

Published by Abdo Kids, a division of ABDO, PO Box 398166, Minneapolis, Minnesota 55439.
Copyright © 2018 by Abdo Consulting Group, Inc. International copyrights reserved in all countries.
No part of this book may be reproduced in any form without written permission from the publisher.

Printed in the United States of America, North Mankato, Minnesota.

052017

092017

THIS BOOK CONTAINS
RECYCLED MATERIALS

Photo Credits: Glow Images, Granger Collection, iStock, Shutterstock

Production Contributors: Teddy Borth, Jennie Forsberg, Grace Hansen

Design Contributors: Christina Doffing, Candice Keimig, Dorothy Toth

Publisher's Cataloging in Publication Data

Names: Murray, Julie, 1969-, author.

Title: September / by Julie Murray.

Description: Minneapolis, Minnesota : Abdo Kids, 2018 | Series: Months |
    Includes bibliographical references and index.

Identifiers: LCCN 2016962469 | ISBN 9781532100239 (lib. bdg.) |
    ISBN 9781532100925 (ebook) | ISBN 9781532101472 (Read-to-me ebook)

Subjects: LCSH: September (Month)--Juvenile literature. | Calendar--Juvenile literature.

Classification: DDC 398/.33--dc23

LC record available at http://lccn.loc.gov/2016962469

Table of Contents

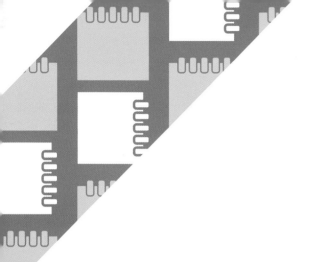

September

There are 12 months in the year.

January

February

March

April

May

June

July

August

September

October

November

December

5

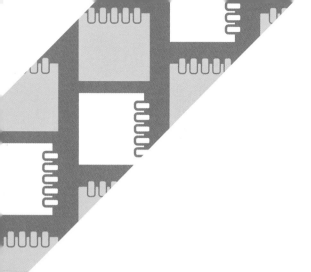

September is the 9th month.

It has 30 days.

September

1	2	3	4	5	6	7
8	9	10	11	12	13	14
15	16	17	18	19	20	21
22	23	24	25	26	27	28
29	30					

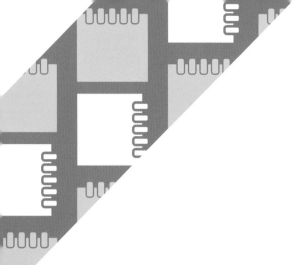

Labor Day is the first Monday.

Cal has a family picnic.

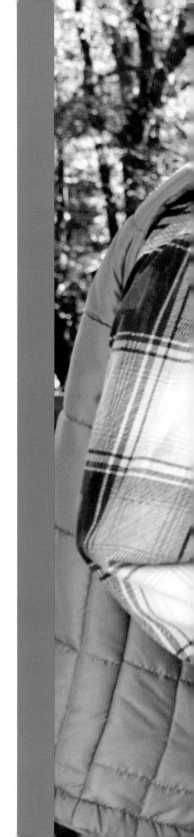

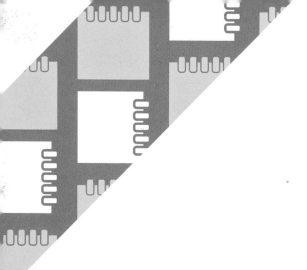

Ben celebrates Rosh Hashanah.

He eats apples and honey.

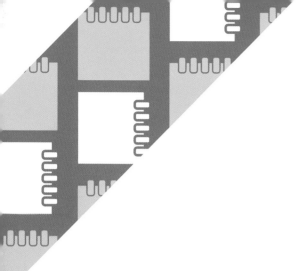

Kids are back in school.

Sam likes his new desk.

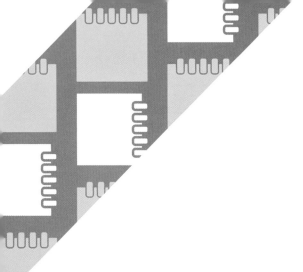

School is fun! Ana gets
to read to the class.

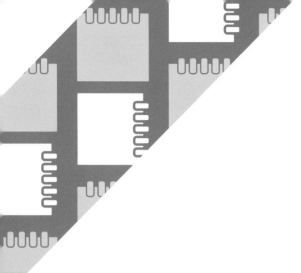

Johnny Appleseed was born in 1774. His birthday is on the 26th!

17

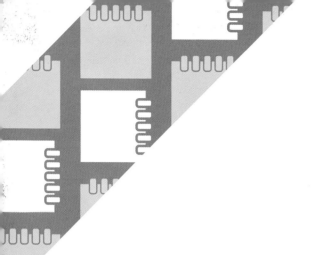

The first day of fall is in September. Oak leaves turn orange.

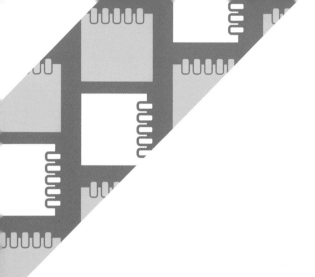

Sara goes on a hike.

She loves September!

Fun Days in September

Newspaper Carrier Day
September 4

International Literacy Day
September 8

Chocolate Milkshake Day
September 12

National Guacamole Day
September 16

Glossary

Johnny Appleseed
(John Chapman) an American gardener who introduced apple trees to many states.

Labor Day
a public holiday that honors working people.

Rosh Hashanah
the Jewish New Year festival.

Index

abdokids.com

Use this code to log on to abdokids.com and access crafts, games, videos, and more!

Abdo Kids Code:
MSK0239

24